IMAGES
of England

CHARLTON ATHLETIC
FOOTBALL CLUB

IMAGES
of England

CHARLTON ATHLETIC
FOOTBALL CLUB

Compiled by
David Ramzan

TEMPUS

First published 1998
Copyright © David Ramzan, 1998

Tempus Publishing Limited
The Mill, Brimscombe Port,
Stroud, Gloucestershire, GL5 2QG

ISBN 0 7524 1504 2

Typesetting and origination by
Tempus Publishing Limited
Printed in Great Britain by
Midway Clark Printing, Wiltshire

Present and forthcoming football titles in the *Archive Photograph Series*:

Bristol Rovers
Burnley
Bury
Cardiff City 1899-1947
Cardiff City 1947-1971
Charlton Athletic
Crewe Alexandra
Crystal Palace
Exeter City
Gillingham
Luton Town
Newport County 1912-1960
Oxford United
Plymouth Argyle 1886-1986
Reading
Sheffield United
Sunderland
Swansea Town 1912-1986
Tranmere Rovers
Wrexham
York City

Contents

The author, about to embark on his life-long devotion to Charlton Athletic.

Introduction

During Charlton's years in exile away from The Valley – ground sharing with Crystal Palace and then West Ham – many prospective young fans were lost. Now the club is well-established back in its spiritual home and there are many newer supporters who are not aware of the club's proud heritage and that there ever was a time when Charlton ran shoulder to shoulder with great names such as Arsenal, Manchester United and Newcastle. Those were the days when Charlton played in Wembley cup finals and were invited to play in tournaments all over the world. I hope that the images in this book will show what a glorious history Charlton have had and that we are not, as many that do not know us say, a small club.

When I first started going to watch Charlton play at The Valley, the names of Seed, Bartram and Welsh were often spoken of by my late father, who went to the ground to support his heroes when he was a boy. It wasn't until much later that I realised how significant these people were in the past glory of Charlton Athletic. He often spoke about the time he was taken on a coach (or charabanc, as they were known then) to see them play Manchester United at Leeds Road in the semi-final of the 1948 FA Cup. This was a time when Charlton Athletic were a major force in English football, a time when crowds at The Valley were in excess of 50,000. My father was one of those boys who were passed down over the heads of the crowd so he could get a better view at the front. Unfortunately, when I started to go to watch Charlton those big crowds had gone and my father had stopped going to games as well. When Charlton returned from their enforced exile in 1992, I had intended to go to a game with him on my fortieth birthday the following year. It was to be the first time my father and I had ever been to a football match together. Two months before this, he was taken ill and did not recover, so we never did get to see a game together at The Valley.

Over the years, Charlton Athletic Football Club has seen many highs and lows but, at last, it seems that glory has come back to the club. Charlton's history has quite possibly been more exceptional and varied than any other club in the League structure: from the team of boys who formed the club, back in 1905, to the members, players, officals and supporters who won promotion to the Premier League at the end of the 1997/98 season.

With a history such as Charlton's, I thought it might be difficult to gather together hitherto-unpublished images, as there have already been several well-produced books on the players and history of the club and I did not want to repeat pictures that have been seen before. With this in mind, I requested help from my fellow supporters to find material especially significant to them, to share their memories of a club we have all supported over the years – one supporter remembers the time Charlton played as an amateur side back in the early 1900s! The pictures and memorabilia in this book have been collected by these fans, some of whom are ex-players, over a period of ninety years and are brought together here with items from my own collection, as well as images obtained from libraries and archives. I have tried to put together a selection that will be of interest not only to established Charlton supporters, but also to more recent followers of the club, as well as football fans in general. This book is not intended to be a definitive history of the Charlton Athletic, but a selection of memories that span the glorious years that the club has been in existence.

One
The First Whistle Blows

At the beginning of the 1900s, the game of football was in its infancy. Within a few years, Charlton Athletic Football Club would form, to become part of this extraordinary spectator sport.

Gazing down from Charlton Heights, above the chalk and sand pits, at the beginning of the twentieth century. Charlton's first playing field can be seen off to the far right, on the shore of the Thames. In the foreground, between the railway arches and the high banking, you will find the site of Charlton's last permanent home – The Valley.

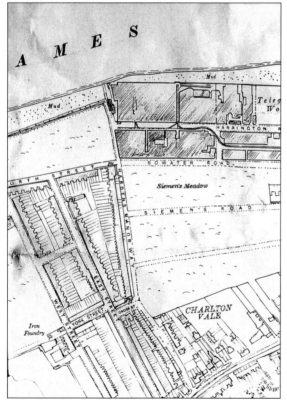

Siemens Meadow was the patch of ground where a group of boys from the local area first kicked a ball under the name of Charlton Athletic in 1905. This map, from the early 1900s, shows the field alongside the Siemens telegraph factory.

The first game ever? An artist's impression of the boys playing a match in their first season. Playing mostly friendly fixtures, the club was so successful that they joined the Lewisham League in 1906.

The first team to wear the famous red and white colours. The boys' average age was fifteen years old. Albert Mills, seen holding the ball, went on to play for Charlton in the Football League in 1921.

The first full season saw Charlton finish top of their division in the Lewisham League, although Siemens Telegraph Works, who owned most of the open space around the area, including the meadow, turned the team off and eventually built over the site. The whole area was to be covered by huge brick blocks of industrial buildings, such as the one in this photograph.

After moving to Woolwich Common, the club went on to play at Pound Park, Charlton, and changed their headquarters from a public house in East Street to the Royal Oak in Charlton Lane. You will still find it packed with Charlton supporters when the team is playing at home.

An area near the Blackwall Tunnel was Charlton's last ground before the move to The Valley. The Angerstein ground is where the team played from 1913 until the First World War; this is now part of the new Millennium site.

Mrs Dorothy Barrom must be the oldest Charlton supporter. Mrs Barrom, now 105, recalls the time she saw the team playing at the Angerstein ground and would be allowed in with a friend for free by the gatekeeper, who normally charged an entry fee. There would regularly be crowds of around 700 watching these matches.

Charlton would move their home ground on several occasions before finding a permanent site. The Charlton sand and chalk pits were a playground for children in the local area, who would dig for fossils and fish in the ponds that formed in the earthworks. Later on, these same children would be shouting and cheering the Charlton team that would soon be playing on this site.

Built in the reign of Charles I, St Luke's in Charlton Village stands high above the site of The Valley. The settlement was a small hamlet at the time The Valley was constructed and many locals helped with digging out the chalk pit to form the pitch.

Opposite the church there was an inn called the Bugle Horn, frequented by supporters. It would be full on matchdays and many older supporters recall the trek down Charlton Church Lane to watch the team play. At this time, football was a new sporting event. Spectator facilities at The Valley were non-existent, but the young children who attended looked on with wonder, as the Charlton team ran out in their bright red shirts and white shorts.

The first match at The Valley was against Summerstown in 1919, Charlton winning the game 2-0. At the end of their first season, Charlton won election to the Kent League.

Pen pictures of the Charlton players became popular with supporters of the day and have now become collectors' items. Charlton were getting a good reputation as they rose through various local leagues, finally becoming professionals in 1920.

Bombed out in the Second World War, the area of New Charlton – where the club was first formed – was a thriving community in the 1920s, full of industrial buildings, shops and Victorian houses. The majority of Charlton fans came from here as the team gained recognition. On joining the newly-formed Southern Football League, they would attract an average crowd of 4,000 spectators.

The following season, after turning professional, Charlton were elected to the new Division Three (South) of the Football League. The first game, against Exeter City on 27 August 1921, attracted a crowd of 13,000. Charlton's line-up for the day was: Hughes, Mitchell, Goodman, Dowling, Hampson, Dunn, Castle, Bailey, Halse, Green and Wilson. Tommy Dowling scored the only goal of the game for Charlton.

An interesting article in *Club Notes* reads 'Ground improvements have been commenced and are being pushed forward as quickly as possible. The ground is being laid out with the idea of obtaining an uninterrupted view of the game and everything possible will be done to study the comfort of those attending matches'. It's taken over seventy years, but at last this goal is now in sight!

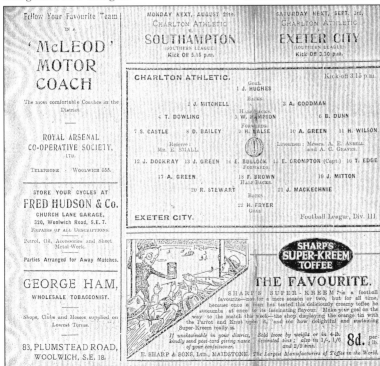

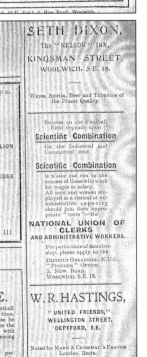

Charlton Athletic 1921/1922 season. From left to right, inserts: Jewhurst, Moody, Upex, Smith, Harbidge, Dowling. Back row: Mr Sullivan (Director), Bacon, Burton, Hughes, Dadley, Bell, Watt. Second row: Hollidge, Castle, Dunn, Goodman, Wilson, Hampson, Cox, Steele, Simons. Front row: Lane, Dodd, Green, Brandon, Walter Rayner (Manager), Purdy, Bowers, Bruce. Seated: Mitchell, Bailey. Albert Purdy visited The Valley after Charlton's return in 1992. He was the only surviving player from the team that played in the Southern League and Division Three (South).

A plan of The Valley and the surrounding area in 1922. The new west stand was completed and it was said at the time that this would make a suitable venue for FA Cup Finals and international matches but, in 1923, after falling attendances, the directors decided to move to a new home at Catford.

A trial fixture at The Valley just before the club moved. It took less than a season before the directors realised the huge mistake they had made and took the club home again. Financially, the whole exercise had been a disaster.

The Mount at Catford, building works preparing the new Charlton ground.

The Charlton team for the 1922/23 season line up in front of the newly constructed grandstand. This campaign saw Charlton go on a famous FA Cup run, beating Northhampton Town (2-0), Darlington (2-1), Manchester City (2-1 away), Preston North End (2-0) and West Bromwich Albion (1-0), before going out at home 1-0 against Bolton, in front of over 41,000.

Two
Onwards and Upwards

A near-disastrous end to a period in Charlton's history saw the club almost drop out of the League in 1926. Gates remained at a good 7,000 average, with the team consolidating in mid-table, during the following season.

Promotion at last – a team line-up from Charlton's promotion season of 1928/29 was: Lindon, Smith, Langford, Hird, Armitage, Pugsley, Wyper, Whitlow, Lennox, Rankin and Horton. When Charlton returned from the away game at Walsall, having won 2-0 to clinch the top spot in their division, supporters filled the streets to greet them home.

The Addicks collectors' card. During one game during that season, the fog was so bad that the crowd lit up newspapers. When a boy asked why this was happening, he was told it was like a fish smoke house (just one more theory on how the club acquired the nickname 'Addicks'). In 1933 the club dropped back into Division Three.

A new manager arrived at The Valley for the 1933/34 season – Jimmy Seed, England international, FA Cup and League title winner. This appointment would be a major turning point in the club's history.

Jimmy Seed made two major acquisitions in the 1934/35 season: a young lad from County Durham called Sam Bartram and Manchester-born Don Welsh. Both of these players became folk heroes at the club. Missing from the line-up is first choice keeper Alex Wright who tragically died in an accident, whilst diving in the sea following a fixture at Torquay United. A supporter recalls attending a reserve game at The Valley the following week and standing for a minute's silence in remembrance before kick-off.

Promotion again, at the end of the 1934/35 season and Jimmy Seed takes the club back into Division Two. Working on a small budget (sounds familiar) and with Jimmy Trotter, Seed's old team-mate, as trainer, they won the Division Three title, finishing eight points clear of second-placed Reading. The following season brought promotion once more.

From Division Three to Division One in two seasons; Jimmy Seed, along with the Charlton team, celebrate after a 1-1 draw with Port Vale at The Valley.

Into Division One and the 1936/37 team line up for the club's historic first season in the top flight. From left to right: Welsh, Tann, Shreeve, Jim Oakes, John Oakes, Bartram, Turner, Robinson, Ford, Prior, Rist, Hobbis, Tadman, Jobling, Williams, Stephenson, Wilkinson, Boulter, Seed (Manager). Arsenal returned to South-east London on 17 October 1936 and, although Charlton lost 2-0, over 60,000 spectators turned up to watch.

S.G. GLIKSTEN.
ROBERT LAW.

A.A. GLIKSTEN.
DAVID. H. CLARK. DR J. MONTGOMERY.

Since the Gliksten brothers had taken control of the club in 1932, Charlton's rise had been monumental. The two brothers invested large amounts in Charlton but were quick to ensure they were paid back as soon as possible. They announced that Charlton would become a major force in Division One, with a stadium to equal Wembley. However, money was not invested, even though the team attracted crowds of over 30,000. At the end of the 1936/37 season, Charlton finished second in the First Division, three points behind Manchester City.

Charlton team group 1937/38. From left to right, back row: Jobling, Turner, Bartram, John Oakes, Welsh, Green. Front row: Tadman, Robinson, Jim Oakes, Owens, Boulter, Hobbis. Charlton kept up their superb performances in the First Division, much to the surprise of the other clubs. A supporter recalls a match at Derby in March 1938 when Charlton, losing 2-0 at half-time, came back in the second half to 2-2, only to be eventually defeated by a late Derby goal – Charlton's players were cheered from the pitch.

F.A. CUP.—FIFTH ROUND

ARSENAL ....0 PRESTON N.E. 1
72,121 £47,210,10,10
Dougal (H.T. 0—0)
BRENTFORD ......2 MANCHESTER U. ...0
27,147—Holliday. £2,021 (H.T. 1—0)
Reid
CHARLTON ATH. ...1 ASTON VILLA 1
•76,051—Robinson •£3,920—Shell
(H.T. 0—1)
CHESTERFIELD ..2 TOTTENHAM H......2
•30,561—Clifton. •£2,627—Gibbons.
Miller (H.T. 0—0)
Sliman †Club's ground record.

A record crowd of 75,031 filled The Valley for Charlton's FA Cup match against Aston Villa, although news reports added an extra 1,000 to the total. Spectators at the game estimated thousands more got in free by climbing over gates and fences. The game finished 1-1, with the replay ending up 2-2, and Charlton finally went out 4-1 in the third match at Highbury.

The 1937/38 season saw Charlton give a creditable performance, finishing in fourth place. The squad, from left to right, back row: Lancelotte, Cann, Wright, Shreeve, Tann, Calland, Davies, Green, Williams. Third row: Owens, Rist, Mordey, Hunt, Hobbins, G. Hicks, Bartram, Thomas, Brown, Stock. Second row: Trotter (Trainer), Jobling, Tadman, Welsh, Mr Clark (Director), Dr Montgomery, Mr Arnott (Director), John Oakes, Robinson, Ford, Hird (Assistant Trainer). Seated: Phillips, Stephenson, Jim Oakes, S.G. Gliksten (Director), Seed (Manager), A.A Gliksten (Chairman). On the floor: Wilkinson, Boulter. The following year, in the last full season before the war, they finished third behind Everton and Wolves, although some unflattering press comments did not give Charlton and Jimmy Seed the credit they deserved.

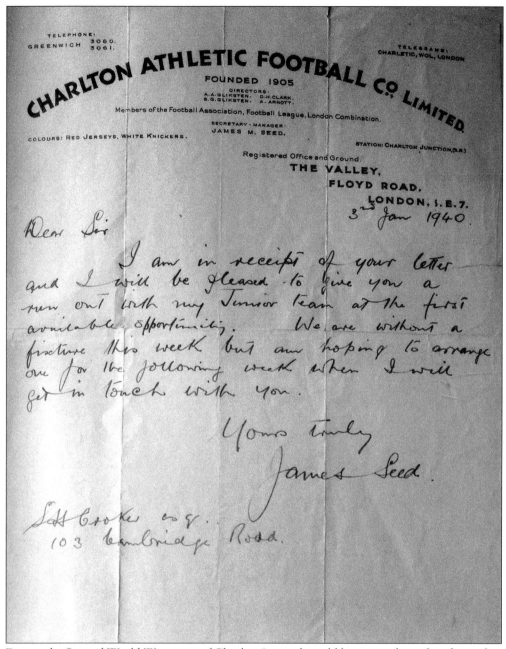

TELEPHONE:
GREENWICH 3060.
3061.

TELEGRAMS:
CHARLETIC, WOL, LONDON

CHARLTON ATHLETIC FOOTBALL CO. LIMITED

FOUNDED 1905

DIRECTORS:
A.A.GLIKSTEN. D.H.CLARK.
S.G.GLIKSTEN. A. ARNOTT.

Members of the Football Association, Football League, London Combination.

SECRETARY - MANAGER:
JAMES M. SEED.

COLOURS: RED JERSEYS, WHITE KNICKERS.

STATION: CHARLTON JUNCTION.(S.R.)

Registered Office and Ground.

THE VALLEY,
FLOYD ROAD,
LONDON, S.E.7.
3rd Jan 1940.

Dear Sir

I am in receipt of your letter and I will be pleased to give you a run out with my Junior team at the first available opportunity. We are without a fixture this week but are hoping to arrange one for the following week when I will get in touch with you.

Yours truly

James Seed.

SH Croker esq.
103 Cambridge Road.

During the Second World War, most of Charlton's squad would be engaged in other duties, but Jimmy Seed was still on the lookout for new players. A young lad's request for a trial resulted in an amateur contract and, after the war, Peter Croker went on to play full-time, making seventy-four appearances for Charlton.

Three
Glory at The Valley

A rain-swept Valley and Portsmouth are the visitors in a match played out with the war not far over the horizon. Don Welsh puts the ball past the Portsmouth keeper, with Harold Hobbis looking on.

A wartime international during 1940 and one of only three occasions on which Sam Bartram would play in an England shirt. Although he never gained a full England cap, a friend of Sam's recalls the time he was called up for a post-war game. Sam, serving in the army at the time, was summoned back to base, losing his England place to Vic Woodley of Chelsea.

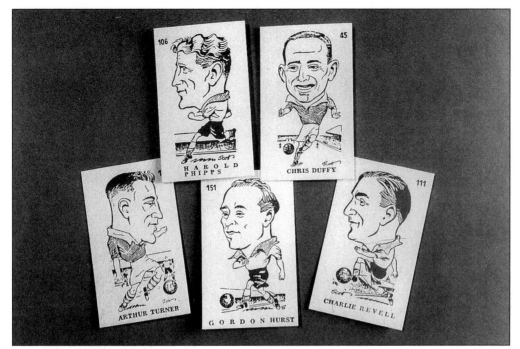

After the outbreak of war, Charlton's players were released from their contracts. The majority of them who were not serving overseas played in a number of games within a reduced League, along with guest star players like Frank Swift, Tommy Lawton and Dai Astley. It would not be too long before Charlton's own stars would feature on collectors' items of the day.

Charlton, playing in the Football League South, entertain Aston Villa in a match that finished 0-0. The vast East Terrace is swelled by hundreds of supporters who managed to get in free.

Charlton's defender, Peter Croker, looks on as an Arsenal player heads for goal. A packed Valley is witnessing Charlton's battle to climb up Division One in 1947. They were at their lowest position since winning promotion.

Sam's ball! Bartram makes sure the opposition can't get onto a through pass. On those occasions when the Charlton defence was breached, the players could frequently rely on Sam to get them out of trouble.

During the FA Cup Semi-final against Newcastle on 29 March 1947, Peter Croker is at hand to back-heel the ball off the line. At least that was how the reports read – Peter recalls that he was just in the right place at the right time and the ball was deflected off his boot!

The ball is on its way into the Newcastle goal. Half of Charlton's team were suffering from food poisoning when the game was played at Leeds and, although the general consensus of opinion was that Newcastle would run out easy winners, Charlton won 4-0 to reach their second FA Cup Final in two years (see chapter six – 'Charlton at Wembley')

Peter Croker can't do anything about this shot as it skims past Sam Bartram. In Charlton's cup-winning season, the Valley crowd averaged over 30,000. The club was one of the best supported in the League at this time.

The Charlton reserves line up for the match against Eastbourne in the 1946/47 season. It was a run out for Peter Croker, who had just returned from injury after breaking his leg in the previous season, missing Charlton's first FA Cup Final at Wembley in 1946.

Harold Phipps goes up with Sam Bartram and a Wolves forward to clear the ball. High above, some of the crowd are standing on top of the garden walls that back onto the East Terrace, in order to watch the game. It wasn't uncommon for them to have water thrown over them by the occupants, who took exception to supporters using their property as a vantage point.

The Brentford 'keeper takes a dive in the mud. Compared to today's playing surface, the Valley pitch would often be devoid of grass: reserve games and training two or three times a week took their toll.

Peter Croker wore the red Charlton shirt with distinction for five seasons. Playing in the right-back position between 1945 and 1951, his older brother, Ted, played centre half during the 1950/51 season. Ted went on to become secretary for the FA. Peter's loyalty was such that he missed out on an England cap against France when he was needed by Jimmy Seed to play in a vital Charlton match.

The famous Charlton Athletic FC newspaper artist, Harold Gittins, produced this team line-up in tribute to Charlton's achievements in the FA Cup and the League during the glory years.

Welsh, Tadman and Robinson show off the kit that was worn in the 1946 FA Cup Final. Although the famous shield-and-robin badge is easily recognisable as being the club logo during the Jimmy Seed era, it was only used for a brief period.

Charlton line-up for a game at Aston Villa on 19 October 1946. Bill Robinson, left of the first row, had only played his debut game a few weeks earlier. He went on to score thirteen goals that season, helping Charlton avoid a relegation struggle.

Talking tactics: Jack Shreeve points out a few manoeuvres to the Charlton team in the directors' tea room (that doubled as a players' ready room).

The gymnasium at The Valley gave the players little room for vigorous exercise. Surprisingly, for a well-established Division One club, the facilities at The Valley had hardly changed from the days in Division Three.

NEW PLAYERS.

At the time of going to press Charlton had only signed two new players, both new to English League football. They are :—

WILLIAM EDWARD KIERNAN, outside left, from Hong Kong ; and NORMAN NIELSON, centre-half or full back, from South Africa.

Kiernan is 23 years of age, stands 5 ft. 8 ins. and weighs 11 st. He was born at Croydon and comes to Charlton from Hong Kong because he took a civil post after being demobbed from the Army, in which he held the rank of Captain. He is not altogether a stranger to Charlton for he put in some training at the Valley at leave periods.

Nielson comes from Arcadia F.C. (Pretoria). He is only 20 years of age, stands 6 ft. 3 in., and weighs 13 stone. Mr. Seed saw him play a number of times in South Africa before getting his signature for Charlton.

Before a new season starts it is expected that further new players will be engaged for with the regular mid-week League games added to the programme this season it will mean that more players will be needed.

In addition to Football League, F.A. Cup, Football Combination and Cup games and Mid-week League, Charlton also hope to provide a regular list of fixtures for a third team. Generally speaking, these will all be played away from home.

JAMES TROTTER
Charlton and England Trainer.

Jimmy was born at Newcastle and served in the R.G.A. in the 1914-18 war, home and abroad. First League club was Bury, with whom he played as centre forward for 2½ seasons. Next he joined Sheffield Wednesday (nine seasons), then followed two seasons with Torquay United. Playing career finished by a knee injury in his first season with Watford. Played alongside Jimmy Seed when with Sheffield Wednesday, and the two Jimmys came together again when Trotter was appointed trainer in season 1934-35.

Fully qualified in every way Jimmy Trotter, who has been described as " almost a doctor," goes about his job in a most painstaking and unostentatious way and his skill alone in the treatment of injuries enables the players to be back again on duty in double quick time.

Has been, and still is, England's first choice trainer and team attendant for the big events.

As a player, Jimmy was a fine goal-scoring centre forward. In season 1925-26 he was leading Second Division goal scorer with 37 goals, and the following season with the same number of goals headed the list of scorers in the First Division.

An article from the official *Charlton Athletic Handbook* on Jimmy Trotter, the club trainer. Jimmy also trained the England national side under manager Walter Winterbottom, Jimmy Seed having put his name forward via Albert Gliksten, who was a friend of Sir Stanley Rous.

Two players making sure they keep up with training schedules – Harold Phipps and Charlie Revell take a run across the Valley turf.

The full Charlton squad from the 1948/49 season. The side finished in ninth place, with some memorable results on the way, including wins over Arsenal (4-3), Everton (3-1), Sunderland (4-0) and Manchester City (3-2). Gates had increased steadily, with over 51,000 watching the Arsenal game.

Two young fans, Mary and Bett Barrom, were part of the crowd at The Valley and are seen here dressed up and ready to make their way to Charlton from their home in Woolwich.

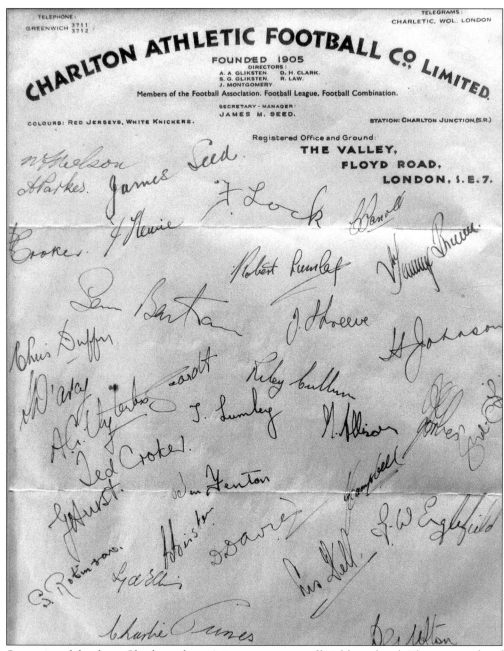

Souvenirs of the day – Charlton players' signatures on an official letterhead. The autographs of the stars of the Cup Final and Division One were as collectable as those of players in the top Premiership sides are today.

Sam Bartram clears his area with a punch upfield. Jim Sanders, Bartram's understudy who never made an appearance for Charlton, complained that Sam would have to die before he ever got in the first team. Sanders eventually left the club to go to West Bromwich Albion.

Charlie Revell and Harold Phipps can't stop the Spurs forward from getting a header at goal. Charlton's fortunes took a downward turn towards the end of the 1940s. With crowds reduced to around 30,000 and without financial investment by the board, Jimmy Seed had to go on with the bold band of players that had served him so well over the years.

Newcastle at The Valley, with Frank Lock and Harold Phipps cutting out a promising attack. Lock was a superb left-back, appearing in over 200 matches. Charlton won this game 6-3, with Lock playing out of position due to an injury that he had sustained.

Charlton in away kit at Aston Villa, 1948. From left to right, back row: Trotter, Fenton, Shreeve, Bartram, Lock, Phipps. Front row: Hurst, O'Linn, Vaughn, Revell, Brown, Duffy.

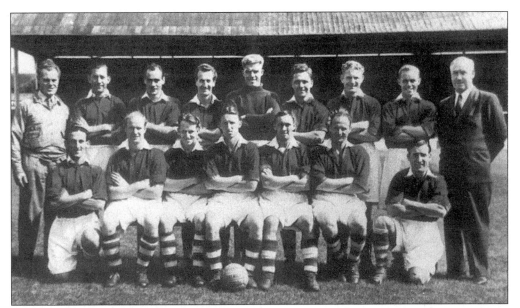

The first team from the 1949/50 season. From left to right, back row: Trotter (Trainer), Revell, Campbell, Brown, Bartram, Lock, Phipps, Johnson, Seed (Manager). Front row: O'Linn, Hurst, Lumley, Vaughan, Purves, Duffy, Fenton. An unusual event occurred before a crucial match against Birmingham during this season. Sam Bartram was the recipient of an anonymous telegram, informing him of how Gill Merrick (the Birmingham 'keeper) could be easily beaten by shooting along the floor. Armed with this advice, Charlton went on to win 2-0. At the end of the season Charlton finished three places from the bottom and Birmingham went down.

Commanding his area, Sam Bartram collects the ball as a packed East Terrace looks on. The team were still struggling well into the 1950/51 season, winning only five out of the first twenty-five matches.

Jimmy Seed signed Swedish international Hans Jeppson to get them out of relegation trouble in 1951. Although he played in only eleven of Charlton's remaining fifteen games, he scored nine crucial goals. Jeppson became a cult hero of the day, a hat-trick in the 5-3 defeat of Arsenal at Highbury confirming his status amongst the fans. Jeppson fulfilled his mission, as Charlton finished sixth from bottom.

Eddie Marsh, Sam Bartram's understudy for five years, finally makes his debut against West Bromwich Albion on 18 November 1950 at The Valley, a game which Charlton lost 3-2. After three more games, Bartram would return from injury and Eddie Marsh would have to wait five more seasons before he became Charlton's number one 'keeper.

Charlton playing Arsenal at Highbury on 13 March 1952. This match marked a record-breaking 418 club appearances for Sam Bartram, but ended 2-1 to Arsenal.

A team line-up from the 1950/51 season. From left to right, back row: Lock, Croker, Bartram, Allison, Jeppson, Johnson. Front row: Hurst, Evans, Vaughan, Fenton, Kiernan, Phipps.

Safe hands – Sam Bartram gathers up the ball. Always a firm favourite with the crowd both home and away, Sam's other talent was his singing and he regularly entertained supporters at their meetings in the Royal Oak.

Four

The End of an Era

Sam Bartram making a save against Arsenal at Highbury. The 1950s saw mixed fortunes for the club. After dicing with relegation in 1951, Charlton finished in the top half of Division One in 1951/52, 1952/53 and 1953/54, but in the bottom half in 1954/55 and 1955/56 – Sam Bartram's last season at the club.

Unusual training techniques as Sam Bartram and new signing Stuart Leary try to out-jump each other. Leary joined the club from South Africa in 1950, playing his first match, against Huddersfield, on 1 December 1951.

An FA Cup tie at The Valley against Blackpool on 6 January 1951. Charlie Revell is scoring from the spot to give Charlton a 1-0 lead. Stan Mortenson hit an equaliser for Blackpool towards the end of the game, that finished 2-2.

Syd Jordan's illustrated view of the Blackpool match.

The Robins, Charlton Athletic's supporters' club, get ready for the trip to Blackpool for the replay. It would not be unusual for the supporters to sleep overnight on the coach for the further away matches.

Team line-up from the 1951/52 season. From left to right, back row: Hammond, Campbell, Evans, Bartram, Hewie, Ufton. Front row: Hurst, O'Linn, Fenton, Leary, Kiernan. Bill Kiernan, a midfielder who scored ninety-three times for the club, was a favourite of many supporters. In one game against Huddersfield, he opened the scoring in the seventy-fifth minute and the game finished 4-0 to the Addicks.

A Charlton victory over Fulham, as illustrated by Harold Gittins, 29 December 1951. Chris Dufty tormented Fulham's defence that day with a marvellous dribbling display, beating three defenders to centre for Riley Cullum to score. Dufty also made the last goal, sending over a great cross for Cullum to score his second and Charlton's fourth.

Charlton fans cheering on The Addicks at Craven Cottage during a match against Fulham.

Charlton's three goalkeepers make light work of a run up the south terracing. They are Frank Reed, Sam Bartram and Eddie Marsh. Eddie recalls that there was no specialist goalie training and 'keepers at the time were very much left to make it up themselves.

54

A Charlton line-up from the early 1950s. An unusual face in the team is goalkeeper Albert Uytenbogaardt from Cape Town, who played just six times during three seasons at Charlton. From left to right, back row: Trotter (Trainer), Fenton, Campbell, Walls, Uytenbogaardt, Phipps, Lock, Johnson. Front row: Hurst, Lumley, Vaughn, Evans, Kiernan. Fans recall giving Albert the nickname 'Humphry Bogard', which was much easier to call out from the terraces.

Three young supporters dressed in their team's colours. The supporters' club would often organise trips to away matches. Iris Hemmings (left) and Jean Tindell (right), recalls one trip to Bolton Wanderers when the coach driver took too many pints of northern beer and was unable to drive back after the match.

A reserve match – Charlton against Queens Park Rangers at a deserted Valley in 1951. While the first team were playing away, the second team would play their home fixtures at the ground.

Severe weather at a snowbound Valley would mean no play on this occasion. In the background you can just make out the original main gates leading out into Floyd Road. The new club superstore now stands on this spot.

Training in Charlton's cramped gymnasium. A prospective Charlton player in the making shows the players his football skills.

Sam Bartram at a presentation for his manager. Sam had been at Charlton almost as long as Jimmy Seed. It is stated that the two men had an agreement that Sam would never be dropped from the side and would stand down himself when the time came.

CHARLTON ATHLETIC

Vol. XXI—No. 36   SATURDAY, MARCH 6th, 1954   Price 3d.

v. PORTSMOUTH

CLUB NOTES

Making their second visit to The Valley within six weeks are Portsmouth, who, readers will recall, defeated Charlton here during extra time in the third round replay of the F.A. Cup on January 14. In the next round, Portsmouth had three games with Scunthorpe before they earned a fifth round ticket, and then, after drawing at Bolton, they lost 2—1 to the Wanderers at Fratton Park.

The Charlton and Portsmouth players should be well acquainted with each other by now, for they have played five hours' football together this season (not counting to-day's match). All three games were stylish and thrilling, and we are hoping for another such encounter to-day.

CHARLIE VAUGHAN.

It is almost 12 months since Charlton transferred Charlie Vaughan to Portsmouth, and if Charlie is in the line-up against us to-day he will be accorded a rousing reception by our supporters, who will never forget the great service he rendered the Robins over a period of six years. It will be recalled that Charlie scored two of Portsmouth's three goals against us in the third round Cup-tie at Fratton. Injury prevented his turning out in the replay at The Valley, but he was present, and was warmly greeted by many of his Charlton friends.

WATCH PETER HARRIS.

Throughout the years, Portsmouth have only once been defeated at The Valley in League or Cup, and a player who always seems to do well against Charlton is Peter Harris, the brilliant Pompey outside-right. Peter has been in great form of late, and was selected for the England "B" team against Scotland at Sunderland on Wednesday, but unfortunately, injury prevented him playing.

It was against Portsmouth at Fratton Park on August 25, 1951 that John Hewie made his League debut for Charlton at right-back. Since then, John, at various times, has also played at left-back, centre-half, centre-forward, and inside-left, and is now at right-half. Where would you like to play next, John?

WAY BACK IN 1922.

Only a few of Charlton's supporters here to-day can remember the first meeting of Charlton and Portsmouth, over 30 years ago. It was at The Valley on February 18, 1922, during Charlton's first season in the Football League, they being elected to the Third (Southern) Division.

About 8,000 people watched the play, and it was unfortunate for the Reds — as Charlton were known in those days, that their captain and centre-half, Arthur Whalley, was unable to turn out through injury.

NEXT FIRST DIVISION HOME MATCH, MARCH 20TH

CARDIFF CITY

KICK-OFF 3.15 p.m.

Charlton match programme from the 1953/54 season. It marked Sam Bartram's 500th appearance for the club, on 6 March 1954.

Before the game, Portsmouth captain Jimmy Dickinson presents Sam with a special cake to commemorate this monumental day.

SAM'S DAY

Yes, it was quite a day when Sam Bartram, the great Charlton goalkeeper, celebrated his 500th appearance for the club.

It began happily with a smile from his daughter Moira as he left home on his way to The Valley . . .

Then, captain for the occasion, Sam was first out of the dressing-room.

A magazine article feature on Sam's record League match. Charlton won the game 3-1. Eddie Firmani scored one goal and Stuart Leary two, making it the perfect day for Sam Bartram and the Charlton fans.

The famous Charlton Athletic make it onto the cover of the *Sport Express*, even though the season did not go well. Falling crowds and a loss of some of their best players meant that the club could only finish in fifteenth place in Division One. From left to right, back row: O'Linn, Hammond, Campbell, Bartram, Hewie, Townsend. Front row: Hurst, Ayre, Ufton, Firmani, Kiernan. The best result that season was a 6-1 win over Aston Villa, a game that saw Eddie Firmani score five goals.

Sam Bartram's last season with Charlton Athletic was 1955/56. From left to right, back row: White, Hammond, Campbell, Hewie, Bartram, Chamberlain, Townsend, Ellis, Ayre. Front row: Hurst, Gould, Ufton, Leary, Ryan, Kiernan. This was a season of mixed fortunes: Sam left the club, Stuart Leary hit twenty-four goals, Charlton celebrated a 3-0 victory over eventual League champions Manchester United, but only finished fourteenth in Division One themselves.

Arsenal were Charlton's opponents on 10 March 1956. Sam Bartram kept goal for the last time, the manager's role at York City awaiting him after his retirement from first-team football. Photographers follow him to the open end of The Valley to get their pictures of Charlton's most famous player.

One more clean sheet in a career at Charlton which spanned twenty-two years. His 623 League and cup appearances remains a club record to this day. Supporters recall how The Valley rose in a chorus of appreciation at the end of the match, which finished 2-0 to the Addicks.

A player's contract from 1955. This yielded a weekly sum of twelve pounds during the season and ten out of season, giving the player at least one year's security. There were no long-term contracts at this time and players like Eddie Marsh were retained from year to year.

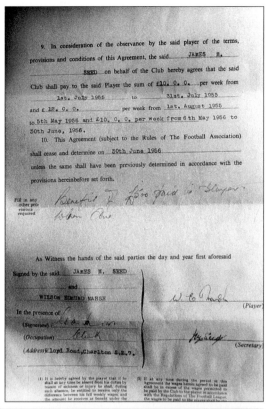

Sitting for a sculpture in the Charlton boardroom. After twenty-three years as manager, Jimmy Seed, at sixty-one, had done more for Charlton Athletic Football Club than anyone could ever have expected. Working with limited resources, he had built a side virtually from nothing to become one of the most successful clubs in English football.

The vote of confidence? Directors toast each other while Benny Fenton, who Jimmy Seed hoped would take over from him when he eventually retired, sits to the left of the group.

First match of the season at Villa Park on 18 August 1956. Aston Villa had been promoted the previous season and Charlton expected to win the match. Villa won the match 3-1, and it started to become apparent that the club was in trouble.

Jimmy Seed and the 1956/57 team at a rather barren-looking Valley. The directors in recent years had not invested adequately in either the team or the ground. After five losses out of five, Jimmy Seed knew he had a problem on his hands. However, he had a good squad of players and was confident of turning the situation around. The directors never gave him the chance. On 3 September he was sacked under the guise that he had retired due to ill health.

Burnden Park, 12 September 1956. This was Jimmy Trotter's first game as official manager. The team on the day was, from left to right, back row: Hammond, Campbell, Marsh, Chamberlain, Hewie, Ellis. Front row: Gould, Kiernan, Hurst, Leary, White. Continuing the form they had shown in the last days of Jimmy Seed, the goals kept going in against them and Charlton lost to Bolton 2-0.

A trip across the Thames for a London derby against Chelsea. Charlton won the match 3-1, but it was only their third win in sixteen games. Eddie Marsh, the Charlton 'keeper, finds himself in the firing line as a weak defence means that he is kept busy.

Division One opposition, such as West Brom, Blackpool and Arsenal, would no longer visit The Valley as Charlton were relegated at the end of the season. The players should not have shouldered all the blame. The directors had been reluctant to release money to strengthen the side and it cost them a place in the top flight (lending strength to the old adage 'you have to speculate to accumulate').

Five

The Game Continues

Back in Division Two, but Charlton can still score goals. An amazing display at home set an all-time record in League history on 21 December 1957.

Johnny Summers hit five in the 7-6 win over Huddersfield. This well-documented match is part of Charlton folklore. Losing 5-1, with the Addicks down to ten men, they put on the most amazing fight-back ever. After pulling the match back to six-all, Charlton's 'Buck' Ryan, hit the winner in the eighty-ninth minute. Fans who were there tell how the crowd erupted – rattles twirled as hundreds of flat cups were tossed into the air.

Finishing third in Division Two, Charlton missed out on going straight back into the top flight. Over the following seasons, Charlton played good football and scored lots of goals but they couldn't quite make it. This is the team getting ready for the 1959/60 season. From left to right, back row: White, Edwards, Werge, Evans. Second row: Trotter (Manager), Sewell, Summers, Duff, Jago, Townsend, Shreeve. Front row: Lawrie, Leary, Hewie, Lucas, Kiernan.

The goals were flying in this season, Charlton hitting the back of the net ninety times in League matches. Unfortunately for Charlton, a record was made away at Aston Villa where they lost 11-1. In the last match of that season, Charlton beat Portsmouth 6-1.

In the 1961/62 season, Charlton legend Stuart Leary had to save the club from the drop into Division Three. After another bad start to the season, Jimmy Trotter was sacked without ceremony and Frank Hill took over. Leary scored seven goals in eleven games, with Charlton winning six of them. They finished eight places from the bottom.

The new look kit for the Addicks in 1964 was all-white with red shoulders and black socks. Unfortunately, the play was much the same and the highlight of the season was Mike Bailey winning his first England cap.

'The Valiants' was a nickname acquired after a competition was held to re-design the club badge. The club carried on with the high turnover of managers after Frank Hill was sacked in 1965. Next came Bob Stokoe, then Eddie Firmani and Theo Foley (who lasted the longest by staying in the post for a little over four seasons until 1974). The team at the start of the 1972/73 season was, from left to right, back row: Flanagan, Clarke, Jones, Dunn, Curtis. Middle row: Foley (Manager), Shipperley, Plumb, Hunt, Reeves, Bond, O'Kane, Horsefield, Murphy (Coach). Front row: Hunt, Ellis, Peacock, Davies, Warman. 'Keeper John Dunn was signed from Aston Villa to replace fans' favourite Charlie Wright.

When Colin Powell joined Charlton they were playing in Division Three. An exciting left-winger, he teamed up well with forward Arthur Horsfield, who netted twenty-five League goals in the course of the 1972/73 season, scoring one himself. At the beginning of the season supporters were at last demanding more from the directors. Some fans recall standing in the Covered End shouting, with others, for Gliksten to resign.

New manager Andy Nelson took over in 1974 and guided Charlton back to Division Two. Before his sacking, Theo Foley had signed Derek Hales, who was instrumental in Charlton's promotion, scoring twenty goals. Once they had regained Division Two status, Charlton hovered around mid-table until the 1978/79 season, when they finished fourth from bottom.

Mike Flanagan scoring his third goal against Spurs (his old club) on 15 October 1977, in a game which Charlton won 4-1. During the match, Mark Penfold broke his leg in an accidental collision so bad that several fans said they could hear the crack as the bone snapped.

Chairman Mark Hulyer takes a gamble in signing one of the most skilful players to turn out at
The Valley. In a reserve match against Swansea City, over two thousand fans turned out to see
the 1977 European Footballer of the year. Derek Hales, in his second period with the club, looks
on. It was the view of at least one fan that Simonsen was always one step ahead of his
team-mates in thought and skill.

Robert Lee, a future England international, scores for Charlton in a season full of incident.
Charlton's latest manager, Lennie Lawrence, took on more than just managing a football team.
At this point the club was deeply in dept with threats of bankruptcy hanging over it. Simonsen
had departed and so had the crowds.

The East Terrace, that once held over 30,000, was now sparsely populated, crumbling and neglected – it mirrored the fortunes of the club at this time.

Alan Curbishley joins Charlton from Aston Villa. Capped ten times for the England youth side and twice for the under-21s, he scored a goal on his home debut against Grimsby Town on 29 December 1984. Alan would win promotion to the top flight with Charlton twice, as a player and then as a manager.

What a superb forward line! On 2 March 1985, Charlton were losing to Barnsley 3-1 at half-time, but came back to win 5-3, the Charlton goals coming from Dowman (2), Moore, Lee and Flanagan. Derek Hales, who came on as substitute, did not get on the score sheet that day.

The Valley before its closure. On 21 September 1985, with rising debts and the East Terrace out of bounds for supporters, the ground was deemed unsafe for public use. The Sunley Group, headed by John Fryer, decided to move the club to Selhurst Park. Michael Gliksten, who still owned The Valley, also wanted part of the land for housing.

Lennie Lawrence wears his diplomat's hat when trying to appease angry fans, but was powerless to stop the move and Charlton's last game at The Valley, against Stoke, took place on 21 September 1985. Mark Stuart and Robert Lee scored the goals in a 2-0 win. Demonstrating fans stayed on the pitch well after the final whistle, many taking bits of the ground and pitch as souvenirs.

Selhurst Park, home of rivals Crystal Palace, was a difficult journey to make through South-East London suburban streets. Many supporters stayed away in protest, even though Charlton, miraculously, were heading for promotion.

Charlton beat Carlisle 3-2 away to win promotion into Division One on 3 May 1986. From left to right, back row: Shipley, Peake, Humphrey, Stuart, Melrose, Jacobs. Middle row: Hall (Physio), Eastick (Coach), Pender, Johns, Pearson, Bolder, Shirtliff, Clarke (Youth Coach), Gallagher (Physio). Front row: Lee, Walsh, Gritt, Aizlewood, Lawrence (Manager), Thompson, Curbishley, Reid.

THE TODAY FOOTBALL LEAGUE

PLAY-OFF FINAL
FOR FIRST DIVISION PLACE—REPLAY

CHARLTON
V
LEEDS

PLAYED AT
THE HOME OF
BIRMINGHAM CITY F.C.
ST. ANDREW'S GROUND
BIRMINGHAM
FRIDAY
29th MAY
1987

★ Official
Programme
Price: 40p

Charlton held their own for most of the season, finishing in nineteenth place to put them into the play-offs. They firstly played Division Two Ipswich, winning 2-1 over two legs, then Leeds United, winning at home 1-0 and losing away 1-0. A final replay at St Andrews saw Charlton hold on to their Division One status by winning 2-1 after extra time.

Final Play-Off Matches

MAY 23rd
V. Leeds United (Home)
Score: 1-0

Bolder - Humphrey - Reid - Peake
Thompson - Miller - Gritt - Stuart - Melrose
Walsh - Crooks - Milne

MAY 25th
V. Leeds United (Away)
Score: 0-1

Bolder - Humphrey - Reid - Peake
Shirtliff - Miller - Gritt - Lee - Melrose
Walsh - Crooks - Pender

MAY 29th
V. Leeds (Birmingham)
Score: 2-1

Bolder - Humphrey - Reid - Peake
Shirtliff - Miller - Gritt - Lee - Melrose
Walsh - Crooks - Stuart

A profile of Charlton's first season in Division One. The team had some notable wins, including Manchester United (away 1-0), Everton (home 3-2), Manchester City (home 5-0), Chelsea (away 1-0) and Newcastle (away 3-0).

TODAY LEAGUE DIVISION ONE
(Up to and including 12th May)

	P	W	D	L	F	A	W	D	L	F	A	Pts
Everton	42	16	4	1	49	11	10	4	7	27	20	86
Liverpool	42	15	3	3	43	16	8	5	8	29	26	77
Tottenham	42	14	3	4	40	14	7	5	9	28	29	71
Arsenal	42	12	5	4	31	12	8	5	8	27	23	70
Norwich	42	9	10	2	27	20	8	7	6	26	31	68
Wimbledon	42	11	5	5	32	22	8	4	9	25	28	66
Luton Town	42	14	5	2	29	13	4	7	10	18	32	66
Nottm. Forest	42	12	8	1	36	14	6	3	12	28	37	65
Watford	42	12	5	4	38	20	6	4	11	29	34	63
Coventry	42	14	4	3	35	17	3	8	10	15	28	63
Man. United	42	13	3	5	38	18	1	11	9	14	27	56
Southampton	42	11	5	5	44	24	3	5	13	25	44	52
Sheffield Wed.	42	9	7	5	39	24	4	6	11	19	35	52
West Ham	42	10	4	7	33	28	4	6	11	19	39	52
Q.P.R.	42	9	7	5	31	27	4	4	13	17	37	50
Newcastle	42	10	4	7	33	29	2	7	12	14	36	47
Oxford United	42	8	8	5	30	25	3	5	13	14	44	46
Charlton	42	7	7	7	26	22	4	4	13	19	33	44
Leicester	42	9	7	5	39	24	2	2	17	15	52	42
Man. City	42	8	6	7	28	24	0	9	12	8	33	39
Aston Villa	42	7	7	7	25	25	1	5	15	20	54	36

SOUTH EAST COUNTIES LEAGUE DIVISION ONE							
Final Table Season 1986/7							
	P	W	D	L	F	A	Pts
Tottenham H.	30	23	4	3	90	25	50
Watford	30	21	6	3	92	32	48
Chelsea	30	19	4	7	65	35	42
Arsenal	30	16	7	7	73	41	39
West Ham Utd.	30	15	3	12	67	66	33
Millwall	30	13	7	10	49	60	33
Portsmouth	30	13	5	12	44	46	31
Norwich City	30	11	9	10	41	45	31
Ipswich Town	30	11	7	12	55	60	29
Charlton Ath.	30	9	9	12	47	48	27
Gillingham	30	8	9	13	51	62	25
Orient	30	8	5	17	53	68	21
Southend Utd.	30	8	5	17	36	61	21
Q.P.R.	30	8	4	18	32	60	20
Cambridge U.	30	4	8	18	32	70	16
Fulham	30	5	4	21	28	76	14

THE FOOTBALL COMBINATION							
Final Table of Results 1986-87							
	P	W	D	L	F	A	Pts
Tottenham H.	38	25	8	5	87	38	58
Chelsea	38	24	8	6	87	33	56
Arsenal	38	23	7	8	77	42	53
Watford	38	22	8	8	81	40	52
Luton Town	38	21	6	11	95	53	48
Norwich City	38	20	6	12	82	63	46
Q.P.R.	38	19	8	11	78	69	46
West Ham U.	38	19	6	13	79	58	44
Swindon T.	38	19	5	14	100	87	43
Charlton Ath.	38	15	10	13	58	59	40
Ipswich Town	38	17	5	16	56	64	39
Southampton	38	16	5	17	66	68	37
Fulham	38	14	8	16	58	66	36
Oxford Utd.	38	10	9	19	63	79	29
Portsmouth	38	11	7	20	50	80	29
Crystal Palace	38	8	11	19	52	73	27
Reading	38	10	4	24	42	95	24
Millwall	38	6	8	24	41	82	20
Bristol Rovers	38	6	5	27	49	104	17
Brighton & H.A.	38	6	4	28	44	92	16

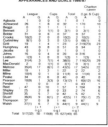

APPEARANCES AND GOALS 1986/87

	League		Cups		Total		Charlton career (Lge & Cup)	
	A	G	A	G	A	G	A	G
Agboola	1	0	0	0	1	0	1	0
Aizlewood	26	1	6	0	32	1	170	10
Beggs	0	0	1	1	1	1	1	1
Bennett	2	0	1(1)	0	3(1)	0	3(1)	0
Bolder	31	0	6	0	37	0	37	0
Crooks	10(2)	2	0	0	10(2)	2	10(2)	2
Curtishley	9(1)	0	3	0	12(1)	0	68(1)	6
Gritt	19	1	4	1	23	2	319(25)	23
Humphrey	43	0	8	0	51	0	94	2
Jacobs	0	0	4	0	4	0	5	0
Johns	16	0	4	0	20	0	316	0
Leaburn	1(3)	1	0	0	1(3)	1	1(3)	1
Lee	31(4)	3	7(1)	4	38(5)	7	116(20)	29
MacDonald	2	0	1(1)	0	3(1)	0	3(1)	0
Melrose	35(4)	17	8(1)	0	43(5)	17	54(5)	22
Miller	19	1	3	0	22	1	22	1
Milne	10(4)	0	1	0	11(4)	0	11(4)	0
Peake	34	0	6	0	40	0	40	0
Pearson	10(9)	1	3(3)	0	13(12)	1	60(12)	16
Pender	1	0	0	0	1	0	43	1
Reid	47	0	10	0	57	1	104	9
Shipley	25	2	8	0	33	2	74	6
Shirtliff	35	5	7	0	42	5	42	5
Stuart	36(4)	9	6(1)	2	42(5)	11	70(17)	25
Thompson	37	0	9	1	46	1	87	1
Walsh	37(1)	6	7	3	44(1)	9	44(1)	9
	(+1 o.g.)		(+1 o.g.)		(+2 o.g.)			
Total	517(32)	50	110(8)	15	627(40)	65		

Charlton Athletic battled on in Division One for another three seasons. By the time the final match of the 1989/90 season came along at Manchester United, Charlton were relegated. Supporters made it a party atmosphere, turning up in fancy dress, but unfortunately the score was 1-0 to United.

A group of fans attending the last away game of the season spend the weekend away, sampling the local hostelries – a tradition they started in Charlton's first season in Division One.

For more than five years, Charlton supporters campaigned to get the club back to The Valley, forming committees of all types, culminating in the Valley Party. This organisation was set up to fight for Charlton Athletic's rights in the local elections and nearly 15,000 votes were cast for their return. Council objections gave way and, at last, Charlton were coming home.

For just over a season, Charlton played at Upton Park, while The Valley was made ready for their return. Lennie Lawrence had left and Alan Curbishley and Steve Critt had taken over as joint managers. A new board of directors, headed by Roger Alwen, were in control of the club. The first game back at Charlton's home took place on 5 December 1992 and Colin Walsh scored the goal in the 1-0 win over Portsmouth.

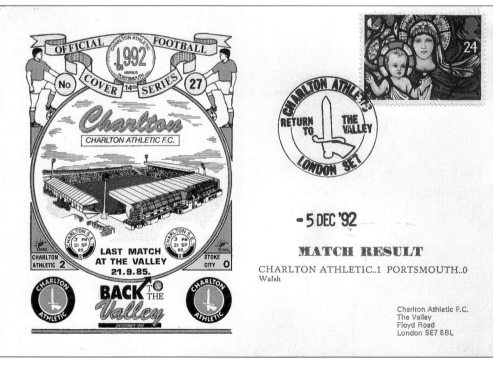

One of many Charlton cup ties against major opposition sees Steve Brown closing in on Ryan Giggs at Old Trafford. In the following four seasons, Charlton went from strength to strength, on and off the pitch. Richard Murray and Martin Simons took over control of the club and Alan Curbishley took sole charge of the team, with Les Reed as his number two.

A limited-edition print of the squad that finished in a play-off in 1987. Charlton lost out to Crystal Palace for a place in the final at Wembley.

Charlton Veterans take on all comers! Keith Peacock, Charlton's long-serving player and now assistant manager, runs the highly successful Veterans side, which consists of ex-Addicks and plays for charities. They remain, to date, unbeaten. Here, Mike Bailey stands off a West Ham forward, while Colin Powell tries to get back into defence.

Six
Charlton at Wembley

During a period of five years, Charlton Athletic appeared in four Wembley Cup Finals, losing two and winning two. By the end of the 1997/98 season, the club would have appeared at the home of football no less than six times.

A collection of Charlton Cup Final programmes from 1943 to 1987. The Charlton *v*. Derby issue has become a very collectable item, along with the two War Cup Final programmes.

In the Football League (South) Cup Final, Arsenal became the first opponents that the Addicks would face at Wembley. In this photograph, the Duke of Gloucester is being presented to the team as Jimmy Seed stands behind captain Don Welsh. The other players are, from left to right: Cann, Revell, Oaks, Brown, Shreeve, Phipps, Mason, Davis, Green, Hobbins. The final score was 7-1 to Arsenal.

Back to Wembley for the 1944 League Cup (Southern) Final. A wartime crowd of 85,000 attended the match when Charlton played Chelsea on 15 April 1944.

Charlie Revell scores one of his two goals in the 1944 final. Charlie was a player who could do well in any position on the field, scoring 100 goals in his football career. He hit six goals against Luton Town at The Valley on 28 October 1944, a game which finished 9-4 to the Addicks.

The cup is won as Charlton beat Chelsea 3-1 and take their first major trophy back to The Valley.

Charlton missed out on a Wembley appearance in 1945 but were back for the 1946 FA Cup Final. A team line-up from that season includes Peter Croker, who in fact broke his leg at The Valley ten days before the match against Derby.

King George is introduced to the Charlton players. Peter Croker, with his walking stick, is shaking hands with the monarch. The team for the day was: Bartram, Phipps, Shreeve, H. Turner, Oakes, Johnson, Fell, Brown, A. Turner, Welsh and Duffy.

Arthur Turner, an amateur player for Charlton, misses the ball with Derby 'keeper Woodley well out of his area.

Don Welsh puts pressure on the Derby 'keeper. This final was quoted as being one of the most bitterly fought in history. The score stood at 0-0 until just ten minutes from time when Derby scored their first goal – although in fact it was not scored by a Derby player, but was an own goal from Charlton's Bert Turner.

Within a minute Bert Turner had scored again, this time in Derby's goal. The match went into extra-time, with Derby finishing as 4-1 winners.

The club were not disheartened by the loss, Jimmy Seed assured his players that they would win the FA Cup next season. A banquet was held in the Cafe Royal for Charlton's beaten finalists and was, by all accounts, a very memorable affair.

Welsh Can Win Cup For Charlton

WHITTAKER'S BIG TEST

By BERNARD JOY

WEMBLEY experience gained last year as runners-up to Derby County, and in 1944 and 1945 in South Cup Finals, should enable Charlton to beat Burnley tomorrow.

They would thus emulate the performances of Manchester City, in 1934, and Preston, in 1938, by winning the FA Cup on reaching the Final for the second successive season.

Only four Charlton players—Croker, Whittaker, Hurst and Dawson—have not relayed at Wembley before. None of Burnley's team has ever appeared there.

My own feeling, gained from two war Cup Finals with Arsenal, is that the preliminaries and atmosphere that make the Wembley occasion are liable to put even the seasoned campaigner off his game.

On Wembley's luxuriant turf, the feel of the pitch and the bounce of the ball are very different from that on today's worn grounds; and they cause those initial unsetting mistakes.

League form, although not a reliable guide to a Cup-final result, favours Burnley, who seem certainties for promotion from the Second Division.

Built round the captain and centre-half, Alan Brown, their defence is their strong point. Yielding only 24 goals in 35 matches—the best record in the Football League—it commands respect from any opposition.

On the other hand, Charlton have had a disappointing season in the League. Indeed, with only six points lead of Brentford and six matches to go (five of them away), they are still in the relegation zone.

But Charlton, in the Cup, are a different side entirely, and their record, to my mind, is superior to that of Burnley.

True, they have had the luck of the draw, being away once only and have come through each round first time. Burnley have been drawn twice away from home, and have had three replays.

Charlton's victims include renowned Cup fighters in West Bromwich, Blackburn, Preston and Newcastle, who together have won the Cup 14 times. Of Burnley's opponents, only Aston

Villa were previous holders, and they share with Burnley the record total of six times.

Main Charlton hope for outwitting the sound Burnley defence is wily Don Welsh—not merely as an opportunist in the penalty area, but also as the general behind the raiding forwards.

That is why he is retained at inside-left and the inexperienced Bill Whittaker, playing his first Cup-tie, is drafted in as deputy to the injured Revell. Duffy on the wing, will have to be at his best to outwit Woodruff, reputed in some influential quarters to be the best full-back in the country.

Welsh's headwork, especially his cross-pass from corners to the opposite goalpost, and Bill Robinson or Dawson, will be a source of danger.

I expect the keen tackling of Johnson and Whittaker to be a decisive factor in dominating the midfield exchanges.

Burnley will rely on goals from the hard-working Morris, alternate-hunt, the opportunism of centre-forward Harrison and the speed on the left wing of Peter Kippax, their amateur international.

Charlton : Bartram ; Croker, Suzeve; Johnson, Phipps, Whittaker ; Hurst, Dawson, Robinson (W), Welsh, Duffy.

Burnley : Strong, Woodruff, Mather ; Attwell, Brown, Bray ; Chew , Morris, Harrison, Potts, P. P. Kippax.

SOCCER TOMORROW

(Kick-off 3.0 except where stated)

F.A. CUP FINAL—Burnley v Charlton Athletic (Wembley).

FIRST DIVISION—Arsenal v Grimsby (3.15), Aston Villa v Blackburn Rovers v Stoke City, Brentford v Middlesbrough (3.15), Derby County v Leeds United, Everton v Preston North End (3.15), Huddersfield Town v Sheffield United, Portsmouth v Manchester United, Sunderland v Bolton Wanderers (3.15), Wolverhampton Wanderers v Chelsea.

SECOND DIVISION—Bradford v Tottenham, Hotspur (3.15), Bury v Nottingham Forest, Chesterfield v Newcastle United (3.15), Fulham v Birmingham, Luton Town v Leicester City v West Bromwich Albion, Town v Coventry City (3.15), Millwall v Swansea Town (3.15), Plymouth Argyle v Birmingham City v Sheffield Wednesday (3.15), Newport County v West Ham United v Barnsley.

THIRD DIVISION SOUTH—Aldershot v Crystal Palace (3.30), Bournemouth and Boscombe Albion v Leyton Orient (3.15), Bristol City v Southend United (3.15), Cardiff City v Ipswich Town (3.15), Exeter City v Mansfield Town (3.15), Northampton Town v Reading, Norwich City v Watford (3.15), Notts County v Walsall, Port Vale v Bristol Rovers (3.15), Swindon Town v Queen's Park Rangers (3.15).

Charlton, struggling in the League, were looked upon as underdogs against Division Two leaders Burnley for the forthcoming FA Cup Final. Bernard Joy, writing from experience having played for Arsenal against Charlton in the 1943 War Cup Final, has another view of how the match will turn out.

BARTRAM
Goalkeeper.

CROKER
Right Back.

SHREEVE
Left Back.

JOHNSON
Right Half.

PHIPPS
Centre Half.

REVELL
Left Half.

HURST
Outside Right.

DAWSON
Inside Right.

ROBINSON
Centre Forward.

WELSH
Inside Left.

DUFFY
Outside Left.

SEED
Manager.

The Addicks were back at Wembley in the 1947 FA Cup Final. Peter Croker was back in the side but Charlie Revell lost out, due to an injury sustained in a match at Portsmouth. Charlie had also missed the previous final.

The Charlton players enjoyed a relaxing break at Eastbourne, staying in the Queens Hotel before the final. There was no clothing sponsorship in those days and most players wore garments off the peg.

The Wembley crowd await the kick-off on 26 April 1947. Over 98,000 saw Charlton and Burnley play ninety minutes of deadlocked cup football to finish with a 0-0 scoreline.

Into extra-time and Charlton go one up when a Don Welsh header finds Charlton's Chris Duffy just inside the penalty area who, hitting the ball first time, sent it flying into the Burnley net.

Sam Bartram keeps Charlton's goal safe while Peter Croker backs him up just in case.

Jack Dunkley's illustration of the final, with goalscorer Chris Duffy as its centrepiece. Many claimed that this was one of the dullest Wembley finals for years – but who cares when you've just won the FA Cup!

The Charlton Athletic team were in their glory years. The pinnacle of Jimmy Seed's reign as manager came with the FA Cup trophy, won by a team of hard-working, highly-talented players.

F. A. CUP WINNERS, 1946-7.

Charlton's cup-winning team, as illustrated by Syd Jordan, included Charlie Revell, but his place on the day was taken by Bill Whittaker.

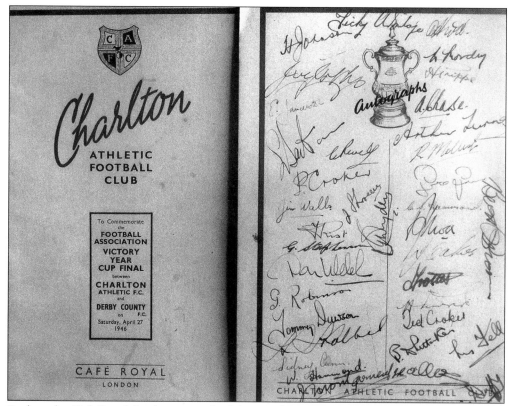

Back to the Cafe Royal for the winners' celebration banquet. A menu for the day was signed by the Charlton Athletic squad.

A crowded Cafe Royal. Players and officials enjoy a successful afternoon's work. At the time, Arsenal and Tottenham were the only other two London clubs to have won the FA Cup.

Floyd Road, Charlton, SE 7. Charlton players show off their prize as the team bus takes them on a tour of the local area. One supporter, a young girl at the time, recalls you could have your photograph taken with a player for one shilling or for two shillings with the cup!

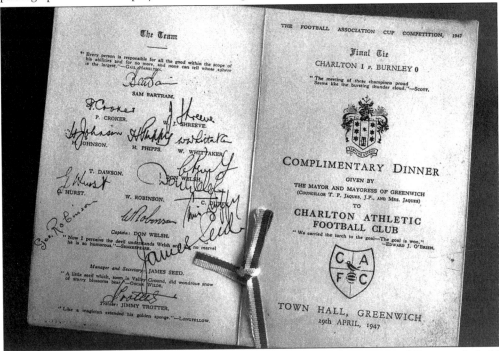

A menu from the complimentary dinner given by the Mayor and Mayoress of Greenwich, held at the town hall on 19 April 1947. The dishes served were named after Charlton players and famous quotations were used to describe the team and management. 'Every person is responsible for all the good within the scope of his abilities and for no more, and none can tell whose sphere is the largest' (Gail Hamilton) for the team and 'A little Seed which, sown in Valley Grounds, did wondrous snow of starry blossoms bear' (Oscar Wilde) for Jimmy Seed.

A girl piper band parade the cup at The Valley in front of a crowd of 45,000 fans. Charlton still had six matches left that season and were near the bottom of Division One. One win and four draws from the remaining games kept them up.

The cup in safe hands. Before the reception, Jimmy Seed managed to drop the cup and damage it. After it had been repaired it was taken back to his home where his daughter, Gladys, and her friend took the opportunity to have their picture taken with it.

Peter Croker's cup-winners' medal, along with an FA Cup Final programme and ticket. It would be another forty years before the club returned to Wembley for another final.

'We're on our way to Wembley' – Charlton win through to the Full Members' Cup Final, against Blackburn on 29 March 1987. A group of supporters are ready for the big day: Norman Billingsley, Geoff Billingsley, Jim Welch, Dave Headley, David Ramzan, Andy Billingsley, Steve Mc Hattie, Alan Armstrong and Christine Woods

A modest attendance of just under 44,000 watched Charlton take control of the match, but they just couldn't find the back of the net. With extra-time beckoning, Colin Hendry took one of Blackburn's few chances and scored.

Robert Lee takes on Blackburn's David Mail to try and get the equalizer, but at the final whistle it remained 1-0 to Rovers. Five Wembley appearances for Charlton Athletic had so far produced a record of lost, won, lost, won, lost.... perhaps a sixth time would be lucky?

Despite the disappointment of losing, fans can celebrate Charlton's return to the big time. For one supporter (wearing the tall hat) especially so, as it was the day that he met his future wife.

Seven
World Travellers

In the 1930s, top European teams would invite leading British football clubs to play exhibition games abroad. As Charlton's fame spread, they were asked to play games in most of Europe and America. Their first match was against the French national side in 1937. Naturally, Charlton won 5-2.

A tour of the USA and Canada was arranged, with Charlton playing thirteen matches in a month. The club sailed off on the *Empress of Australia* on 19 May 1937. In the first game, against the American national side, Charlton draw 1-1. After that match they won every game.

Jimmy Seed is made an honorary Indian chief during a match against Saskatoon in Canada, beating the local side 12-2. The ball was presented to the Indian tribe.

Charlton travelled to France to play Racing Club de Paris at the Colombes Stadium, Paris, on 22 May 1946. The team line-up for the day was, from left to right, back row: Welsh, H. Turner, Hobbis, A. Turner, Phipps, Johnson, Bartram. Front row: Robinson, Tadman, Revell, Duffy.

Sam Bartram can't get to this one as Racing Club score past the Charlton 'keeper. However, the final score is 6-2 to the Addicks (Tadman and Welsh each scoring twice with Turner and Revell getting one goal apiece).

The teams line up for national anthems at the Parc des Princes Paris on 1 January 1947. Charlton played Stade Francais there, in front of a crowd of 20,000.

Peter Croker looks on as Stade Francais score against Charlton. The final result is a 2-2 draw, with Bill Robinson hitting two for Charlton.

The tour of South America in 1954 turned into one of the worst overseas experiences. Although promised a luxurious itinerary by their guests, the team were put into a very drab hotel – The Ecuador – and left to themselves. The rooms were poor and resembled small dormitories.

Sam Bartram sent a card to friends back in Greenwich which read: 'Dear John and Phyll, This is the biggest and best hotel here, needless to say we are not staying there. It is the worst tour I have been on, but I suppose I shall have to make the best of it. Scores to date played 2 drawn 2. Cheerio yours Sam'.

The players and officials boarding the aircraft for a flight in South America. It was an old twin-propeller plane and the players were not at all confident of its air-worthiness.

An official reception held by Charlton's hosts on the South American tour. In all, Charlton played seven matches, drawing three, losing three and winning one – a game that was hastily arranged so the South American officials could make extra money out of the tour.

Eddie Marsh pushes the ball wide of the goal as John Hewie looks on. In a two-match tour of Ireland in 1956, Charlton draw with Shamrock Rovers 2-2 and then went on to beat Waterford 3-2. The European Cup was in its first season and the hope that Charlton would play in a full competition such as this disappeared as they dropped down the League.

The only official European Cup competition Charlton appeared in was when they won through to the finals of the Anglo-Italian Cup in the 1993/94 season. Here, Charlton fans are enjoying the hospitality of an Italian bar.

Ancona scopre che c'è ancora Carruezzo

Ancona	1
Charlton	1

(primo tempo 0-0)

MARCATORI: 3' st Carruezzo, 15' st Leaburn.

ANCONA: Armellini, Fontana, Cangini, Arno, Mazzarano (dal 15' st Vecchiola), Brugnera, Turchi, Ragagnin (dal 1' st De Angelis), Carruezzo, Hervatin, Caccia. (12 Nista, 15 Bertarelli, 16 Varini). All.: Guerini.

CHARLTON: Salmon, Brown (dal 45' s.t. Linger), Minto, Garland, Chapple, Balmer, Grant, Pitcher, Bailey, Nelson (dal 12' s.t. Leaburn), Walsh. (12 Sturgess, 13 Vaughan, 15 Rufus). All.: Gritt e Gurbishley.

ARBITRO: Wilkie (Inghilterra).

NOTE: serata umida, spettatori 2 mila circa con larga rappresentanza inglese. Angoli: 6-3 per il Charlton. Ammonito: Carruezzo.

ANCONA — Al battesimo internazionale dello stadio del Conero rispondono soltanto duemila spettatori ma stavolta ha ragione chi resta a casa perché lo spettacolo è tutt'altro che esaltante. L'Ancona va in campo con le seconde scelte ma Cangini, Ragagnin e Carruezzo danno l'impressione di pensare più a un possibile trasferimento che potrebbe arrivare dalle ultime ore del calciomercato che alla partita. Gli inglesi invece tengono parecchio a questo appuntamento tanto che un centinaio di tifosi ha addirittura attraversato l'Europa per seguire la squadra. Il Charlton si presenta con il classico 4-4-2 con la difesa schierata in linea: il giocatore più interessante è l'ala destra Grant che Cangini non riesce ad arginare. La supremazia territoriale della squadra ospite è evidente nella prima fase della gara mentre l'Ancona opera in contropiede ma solo Hervatin e Caccia sono all'altezza degli avversari. All'11' Walsh serve Gardland il cui diagonale è deviato in angolo da Armellini. Al 15' Grant va sul fondo e serve un pallone d'oro a Balmer che manca la sfera da pochi passi. Nel finale del primo tempo si vede l'Ancona: prima Hervatin conclude alto dalla distanza, poi lo stesso centrocampista sfiora il palo con un diagonale su bel passaggio di Caccia.

La gara si anima all'inizio della ripresa: al 3' Turchi va in pressing su Chapple, ruba palla, cross dal fondo per Carruezzo e comoda conclusione dell'attaccante da due passi. Ancona in vantaggio e vicina al raddoppio: colpo di testa di Turchi alto sulla traversa. Ma al 15' il Charlton pareggia: Linger salta un paio di avversari al limite e serve bene in area Leaburn entrato da pochi minuti, il diagonale dell'attaccante di colore s'infila alla sinistra di Armellini. Nell'azione del gol s'infortuna Mazzarano che viene sostituito da Vecchiola.

L'Ancona ha la palla della vittoria a due minuti dalla fine ma Caccia si fa respingere la conclusione.

Mimmo Cugini

Two matches were played in Italy and two at The Valley. The game in Bresia ended in a 3-2 loss and the Ancona match finished 1-1, with Carl Leaburn scoring Charlton's only competitive European goal. An empty Ancona Stadium proves the Italians have not taken the tournament that seriously.

A cutting from the Italian *Gazzetta dello Sport* reporting on Ancona's match with Charlton said it all – '*Arrivederci*'.

Eight
Valley Heroes

While it would take another book to acknowledge all the players who should come under this category, included are just a few who have come top of the list with those who have contributed towards this publication.

Jimmy Seed, Sunderland, 1914. Although he never played for Charlton, without him it's impossible to contemplate where Charlton would be. During his reign as manager he established Charlton Athletic as one of the great teams in English football, challenging the best for top honours in both League and cup competitions. Jimmy's football career was as remarkable as his managerial success. As captain of Spurs he won the FA Cup in 1921 and was capped for England five times, before captaining Sheffield Wednesday to two League titles in 1929 and 1930. Jimmy Seed served Charlton with distinction as manager for twenty-three years.

Sam Bartram holds the record for being Charlton Athletic's longest-serving player. If it had not been for the Second World War, he would have gone on to appear in even more than a magnificent total of 623 League and cup matches. It was said that Sam was the best 'keeper never to have won a full England cap.

Stuart Leary scores again – a Charlton player for eleven seasons from 1951 until 1962, Stuart scored a total of 163 League and cup goals for the club. Had it not been for the fact he was born in South Africa, he would surely have played as England's centre forward. Stuart did, in fact, play for England at under-23 level, but FA rules changed and he became ineligible to play for the national side.

Don Welsh will always be remembered as the captain of Charlton's FA Cup-winning side. During his career with the Addicks, Don played 216 League and cup matches and scored fifty goals – yet he was a player whose career was interrupted by war. As captain of the side that gained promotion from Division Three to Division One in three successive years, Don Welsh spent eight glorious seasons at The Valley.

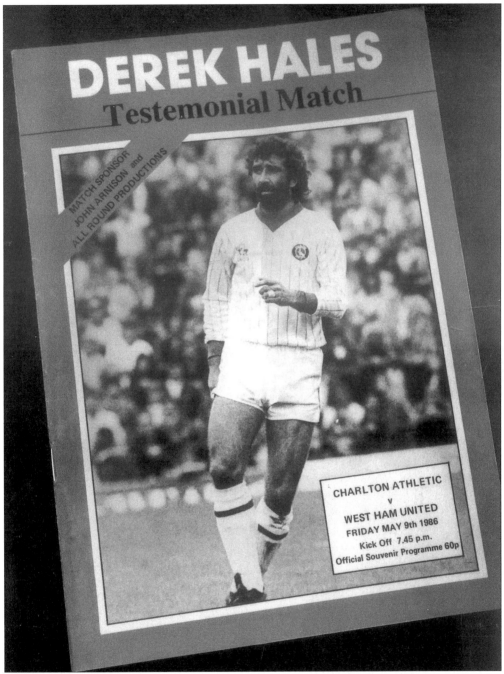

Derek Hales joined Charlton in 1973 and scored on his debut, becoming an instant hit with the fans. An unconventional player, he gained the nickname of 'Killer' through his hard style of play and lethal instincts in front of goal. Never afraid to get in where it hurt, Hales was one of the most feared strikers in the League, scoring a record 168 goals for the Addicks. Derek says he can remember every goal he ever scored and who would want to argue with him!

Forward power – Colin Powell (top left) and Mike Flanagan (top right). Colin joined Charlton in the same year as Hales. Playing on the left wing, his skilful play set up many goals. Mike Flanagan, one of the best footballers to play for the club, hit 120 League and cup goals, whilst making as many as he scored.

Allan Simonsen, the Danish international, only played sixteen matches for the club but was, arguably, the best contemporary player to wear an Addicks shirt. A European Cup winner in 1982 and European Footballer of the Year in 1977, any Charlton fan who saw him play would have been watching the finest and most skilful player in the Football League at the time.

Promotion-winners Alan Curbishley (top left) and Jim Melrose (top right) played their part in the most crucial of Charlton's matches in modern times. Alan Curbishley, an England under-21 and youth player, controlled Charlton's midfield in the 1985/86 promotion season, returning to the club as player/coach and then joint manager with Steve Gritt. As sole manager, Alan took Charlton into the Premier League in 1998. Jim Melrose scored the goals at the end of the 1985/86 season that earned Charlton a place in Division One and scored the only hat-trick for Charlton in their four seasons in the top flight.

Hat-trick hero, Clive Mendonca, hit three in Charlton's play-off final of 1998. Clive notched up twenty-three League goals in his first season with Charlton and was instrumental in winning Charlton a place in the play-offs and then promotion.

Into the Premiership – a limited-edition print of the 1998 play-off winners.

Nine

Back to Wembley and Promotion

With the 1997/98 season coming to a close, expectations amongst the Charlton fans are high –
can Charlton snatch automatic promotion or is it into the play-offs?

Close rivals for promotion, table-toppers Nottingham Forest, visit The Valley in March and are well-beaten 4-2 by the Addicks.

The partly-constructed West Stand, when finished, will take the capacity of The Valley to over 20,000 – enough for the Premier League.

An unprecedented step is taken by the board of directors, when around fifty coaches are paid for by them to take fans free of charge to the Port Vale away fixture on 13 April 1998. 4,000 Charlton supporters travelled to see the team win 1-0.

The players run out at The Valley for the last home game of the season against Tranmere Rovers. It's still tight at the top of the Division One, with only a few points separating the teams.

A crowded East Stand applauds the 2-0 win over Rovers. Charlton have won eight games on the run with a 0-0 draw away at Birmingham on the last day of the season. Eighty-eight points would mean automatic promotion in any other season, but Charlton finished in fourth place.

Alan Curbishley had steered the side into the play-offs for the second time in three seasons and, although bookies favourites to lose out, Charlton beat opponents Ipswich 1-0 at home and away to win a place at Wembley.

Mark Kinsella, Eire international, gets ready at the training ground for the final. New boy Paul Emblen jogs past, as old hand Mark Bright (to the right) contemplates another Wembley appearance. In the background, Mark Bowen, Eddie Youds and Keith Jones take a break.

Final preparations and some ball control practice for Steve Jones, as Alan Curbishley looks on.

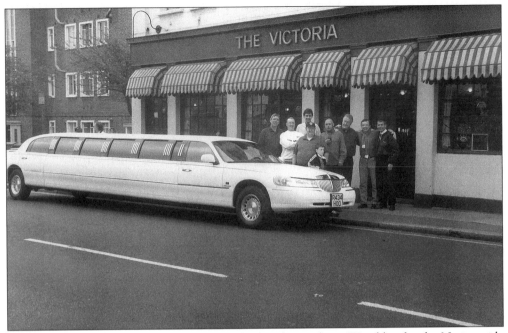

Charlton fans from The Victoria, Greenwich, travel in style to Wembley for the Nationwide Football League Division One Play-off Final on 25 May 1998.

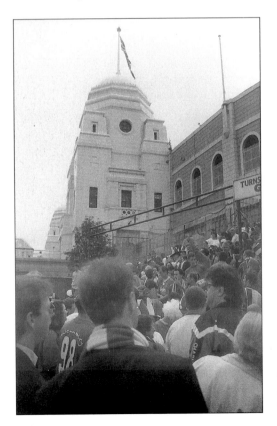

The twin towers – expectations are high as the Charlton fans file in for the game of a lifetime.

Sunderland supporters mix with the Charlton fans at the top of Wembley Way, again the odds are against Charlton to take a place in the Premier League and pundits expect Sunderland to win.

Happy faces and silly hats make this a day to remember, whatever the outcome, in Charlton's most important match since 1947.

A near capacity crowd makes this play-off final a record, with an attendance of 77,739. With 35,000 Charlton fans present, there are over three times more than went to support them in the 1947 FA Cup Final.

The end-to-end thriller is more than can be expected, as two evenly-matched teams battle it out on the pitch, Charlton take the lead, but Sunderland come back and make it 1-1, before going 2-1 up. Charlton hit back with Clive Mendonca scoring his second goal. Then, for the third time in a Charlton final, the ball bursts – the signs are there it could be Charlton's day.

Sunderland take the lead again, but Richard Rufus heads home the equaliser (3-3). In extra-time, one more goal is scored by each side, the match finishing 4-4 – with Clive Mendonca getting his hat-trick – it's now down to penalties.

After five well-converted spot kicks each, it's sudden death – Charlton go into the lead 7-6 and Sunderland must score to stay in the game. They don't and the scoreline says it all – remembering Charlton's greatest comeback against Huddersfield at The Valley. The Charlton fans celebrate as Sasa Ilic saves from Michael Gray and Charlton win promotion to the Premier League.

The play-off final between Charlton and Sunderland is regarded by many to have been the greatest game ever seen on Wembley's hallowed turf. Charlton supporters who saw the 1947 FA Cup Final agree that this game was more important to the club.

A trophy to remember, presented to the 1998 Division One Play-off Final winners – Charlton Athletic Football Club. From a glorious past, we can all look forward to a glorious future.

Acknowledgements

I should like to thank all those who have helped me in gathering together the material for this publication. This collection of assorted images has been collated with the help of friends, supporters, ex-players, club photographers and officials of Charlton Athletic. The majority of the images are of great significance in the memories of the fans that have helped me in this task. I have been a Charlton supporter for over thirty years and have shared many football experiences – both good and bad – with those who have contributed to this book. I should like to thank all those who have supplied photographs, memorabilia and memories, for without their contributions this book would not exist:

David A.A. Ramzan, Jim Jelf, Arthur Jensen , Mick Berry, Percy Castle, John Chadwick, Peter Croker, Keith Ferris, Harry Field, Eddie Goatman, Andy Grierson, Paddy Hawkins, Ernie Hurford, Harold Lugs, Eric Keep, Ken Little, Bob Nokes, Charlie Revell, John Roth, Ken Starkey, Archie Star, Peter Barratt, Bill Swingler, Harry Trew, Dennis Butcher, Frank Beech, Don Freeman, George Daily, Christine Lawrie, Peter Dutton, Gladys Dutton, Jean Tindell, Eddie Marsh, B N Poulter, Tom Morris (Club Photographer), Dorothy Barrom, Betty Reed, Dot Blackwell, Andrew Hawkins, Ron Weston, Lester Trask, Iris Hemings, John Wimbury, Jim Walker, Geoff Billingsley, Gordon Billingsley, Andrew Billingsley, Norman Billingsley, Ray Billingsley, Dave Headley, Steve McHattie, Alan Armstrong, Jim Welch, Mick O'Brien, James O'Brien, Kevin Campbell, Laurie Manchester, Colin Barker, Peter Woods, Fred Clarkson, Reg Malin, Barry Needham, Graham Clark, Alan Russell, Anthony Bristowe, *The Hastings Observer*, Julian Watson and The Greenwich Social History Library, Peter Varney , Roy King, Rick Everitt and the players and officials past and present of Charlton Athletic Football Club as well as Gina Wall for helping me in typing the manuscript.

A particular mention must be made of Colin Cameron, author of *The Valiant 500* and *Home and Away with Charlton Athletic* and also Richard Redden, author of *The Story of Charlton Athletic 1905-1990*, for their help and advice. Special thanks to my wife, Linda, for her help and perseverance while I have been compiling this book. My gratitude goes out to the many individuals and organisations who gave permission to reproduce items in this publication. Finally, I would like to apologize for any inadvertent omissions to the list.